SPORTS FROM COAST TO COAST™

WRESTLING
RULES, TIPS, STRATEGY, AND SAFETY

———— DAVID CHIU ————

rosen
central™

The Rosen Publishing Group, Inc.,
New York

Published in 2005 by The Rosen Publishing Group, Inc.
29 East 21st Street, New York, NY 10010

First Edition

Library of Congress Cataloging-in-Publication Data

Chiu, David.
Wrestling: rules, tips, strategy, and safety / David Chiu.—1st ed.
    p. cm.—(Sports from coast to coast)
Includes bibliographical references and index.
ISBN 1-4042-0187-4 (library binding)
1. Wrestling—Juvenile literature.
I. Title. II. Series.
GV1195.3.C55 2004   J
796.812—dc22   NF

    2003028286

Manufactured in the United States of America

CONTENTS

CHAPTER ONE

Wrestling Throughout History

Wrestling was a highly regarded sport in ancient Rome.

Wrestling is civilization's oldest sport. It is played when two opponents try to pin or hold each other's shoulders on a mat on the ground. The object is to win by pinning the opponent or by scoring the most points through various maneuvers.

The oldest form of wrestling dates from prehistoric times when the sport was a form of hand-to-hand combat. In parts of southern Europe, evidence of wrestling's origins has been found in paintings and carvings in caves. Many of these paintings and carvings date from 20,000 years ago. Artifacts have also shown that wrestling has been around in several ancient civilizations. A portrait of Sumerian wrestlers on stone slabs in ancient Mesopotamia is believed to be 5,000 years old. A small bronze statue of wrestlers was found in the ruins of Khafaji (near present-day Baghdad, Iraq), from 2600 BC. In Egypt, walls of temple tombs dating from 2500 BC show scenes of belt wrestling, an early form of the sport. Aspects of belt wrestling are still used today in modern wrestling.

The ancient Greek poet Homer described a wrestling match in the epic poem *The Iliad*. The match between the Greek warriors Odysseus and Ajax ended in a draw. The struggle between these two warriors is considered one of the world's greatest wrestling stories.

In ancient Greece, wrestling was introduced to the Olympic Games in 708 BC. There were two forms of competition in the games: a toppling event for the best two out of three falls, and pankration, a combination of wrestling and boxing. The most famous of ancient wrestlers of that era—Milon of Croton—won the championship six times. But wrestling was not restricted to those blessed with great physical talents. The Greek philosopher Plato (c. 428–348 BC), then known as Aristocles, was a successful wrestler as a young man.

For a brief time, when the Roman Empire controlled half of Europe in the AD 100s, wrestling's popularity diminished. However, wrestling had made a comeback by the Middle Ages (AD 400s–1500s). In fact it became so popular that some nations considered it a noble sport. In

The Strength of Milon of Croton

The sixth-century BC Greek wrestler Milon of Croton was undefeated in six Olympic championships. How did he condition to hold on to his titles? According to legend, he trained in the off-season for his victories by carrying a newborn calf on his back every day, until it grew into a bull. He was also known for proudly donning his wreaths around his neck as he walked down the streets of his village, to the delight of the townspeople. Unfortunately, though, Milon would die a horrible death: his hand got stuck as he was trying to rip a tree apart. Unable to escape, he was attacked and killed by wolves.

England and France, a champion wrestler was highly prized. In 1520, Henry VIII of England and Francis I of France, both supporters of wrestling, challenged each other to a match. Reportedly, Francis I won.

The Japanese developed a form of wrestling called sumo, which was popular during imperial times (710–1185). In ninth-century Japan, the sons of the late emperor Butonku wrestled to determine who would take over the kingdom. Contestants in sumo weighed between 300 and 400 pounds (136 to 181 kilograms) and wrestled in a circle 12 feet (3.7 meters) in diameter. The goal was to break the opponent down on the mat or pull him out of the ring. Sumo matches were usually over in seconds. This is still practiced today.

Wrestling in North America

Before Europeans began moving to the New World in 1492, Native Americans practiced wrestling. This form of the sport had few rules

Sumo wrestling is a popular sport in Japan, and it hasn't changed much since it was invented during imperial times. In this photograph, taken in 1880, two sumo wrestlers get ready to try pushing each other out of the ring.

and any hold or leverage could be used to win the match, as long as the opponent was pinned on the ground. By the sixteenth and seventeenth centuries, wrestling was a common sport in the colonies of North America. Each settlement had at least one champion wrestler, and contests were held between title holders.

Before becoming president, a young George Washington was a skilled collar and elbow wrestler. Collar and elbow wrestling was a form of wrestling in which each wrestler placed one hand behind his opponent's neck and the other behind his elbow. Later, at the age of forty-seven when he was commander of the Continental army during the American Revolution (1775–1783), he wrestled against various challengers from the Massachusetts Volunteer Infantry.

Future president Abraham Lincoln was a wrestling champion in Illinois around 1830. His approach was catch-as-catch-can, which allowed a wrestler to grab any part of the opponent's body. Other presidents who have wrestled include Andrew Jackson, Ulysses Grant, and Theodore Roosevelt.

Requiring equal amounts of strength and skill, Greco-Roman wrestling has been a popular Olympic event since 1896.

Greco-Roman Wrestling

In the mid-1800s, the Greco-Roman style of wrestling developed in France. Greco-Roman wrestling does not allow holds on the legs or any form of tripping. It is called Greco-Roman because many believe this form of wrestling has existed since ancient times, when the cultures of Greece and Rome dominated Europe. Greco-Roman wrestling was popular in France where public exhibitions were held. However, it didn't gain popularity in the United States. The collar and elbow style was practiced by the troops in the Union army during the Civil War (1861–1865). After the war, wrestlers used to travel across the country competing for prize money. In the 1880s, the catch-as-catch-can style flourished in the United States.

Wrestling and the Modern World

Wrestling became part of the modern Olympics in 1896 in Athens, Greece, when the only style used was Greco-Roman and the only class was heavyweight. Freestyle wrestling was introduced in the 1904 Olympic Games in St. Louis, Missouri. Unlike Greco-Roman, freestyle

Wrestling is a good way for young people to develop physical and mental discipline. In this photo from 1930, a young boy puts his friend in a head-lock while their classmates look on.

allows holds below the waist and on the legs. Since then, there have been both Greco-Roman and freestyle wrestling in the various Olympic weight classes.

Organized wrestling took shape in America when the Amateur Athletic Union was formed in 1888. As the governing body of the sport, it established guidelines, rules, and weight classes. The international organization that sets the rules is the Fédération Internationale des Luttes Associes (FILA), founded in 1912.

In 1903, the Intercollegiate Wrestling Association was formed. It was made up of several northeastern universities, such as Yale, Princeton, and Columbia. This association set the rules for college wrestling. Wrestling programs at colleges such as Iowa State University and Oklahoma A&M (now Oklahoma State) soon took off. In 1928, the National Collegiate Athletic Association (NCAA), the governing body of all college sports, held the first wrestling championship tournament. After World War II (1939–1945), wrestling became a standard part of high school and college athletic programs.

Over the years, wrestling has been universally recognized as a major sport because of its exposure in the Olympics, the Pan American

Added to the Pan Am Games in 2001, women's wrestling has generated a lot of interest around the world. Here, U.S. wrestler Sara McMann (*right*) gets ready to throw Sweden's Sara Eriksson (*left*) to the ground at the 2003 World Freestyle Wrestling Championships in New York City.

Games, and World Championships. These thrilling competitions are full of intensity as the audiences cheer on their countrymen.

Although wrestling has traditionally been a male-dominated sport, women's wrestling has been around since ancient times. It wasn't until the latter part of the twentieth century that it became widely accepted through the World Championships of Freestyle Wrestling and the Pan Am Games. In 2001, the women's competition was finally added to the Olympic Games. It made its debut in the 2004 Olympic Games in Athens, Greece.

American amateur wrestling is governed by USA Wrestling (formerly the United States Wrestling Federation). The organization is responsible for the selection and training of the U.S. teams in international competition. USA Wrestling promotes the sport with activities and programs for various age levels. It charters more than 2,900 wrestling clubs and sanctions more than 1,600 local, state, regional, and national championships.

CHAPTER TWO

How the Sport Is Played

Wrestling is a sport that almost anyone can play. Under wrestling's weight classification system, you compete against someone your own size and weight. Even kids as young as four can wrestle.

Styles of Wrestling

There are three types of wrestling at the amateur level: folkstyle, freestyle, and Greco-Roman. Folkstyle is practiced in elementary school through college. It allows the use of arms, legs, and body to hold opponents above or below the waist. Freestyle is very similar to folkstyle but differs in scoring and strategies. It is most popular in North America. In

This wrestler puts his opponent to the mat with a bone-crushing maneuver.

Greco-Roman style, wrestlers are not allowed to grab the legs of their opponents or use any holds below the waist. This style is practiced mostly in Europe. Most national and international competitions, such as the Pan American Games and Olympics, consist of freestyle and Greco-Roman wrestling. The rules in the major tournaments are different compared to those of high school and college, although the moves are the same.

The Mat

The mat is usually made of foam no more than 4 inches (10 cm) thick and covered in plastic. At the high school level, the mat has a large circle, which is usually 28 feet (8.5 m) in diameter. For college competition, the circle on the mat is 32 feet (9.8 m) in diameter. The larger circle is the wrestling area. Within the larger circle is an inner circle measuring 10 feet (3 m) in diameter, where the competition starts. At the high school level, the inner circle contains parallel starting lines that are 3 feet (1 m) by 12 inches (30.5 cm) from outside to outside. For college these lines measure 3 feet by 10 inches (25 cm). This is where the wrestlers begin their match. There is also a 5-foot (1.5 m) safety area surrounding the larger circle. Wrestlers have to stay inbounds during play and not go beyond the boundary lines; if

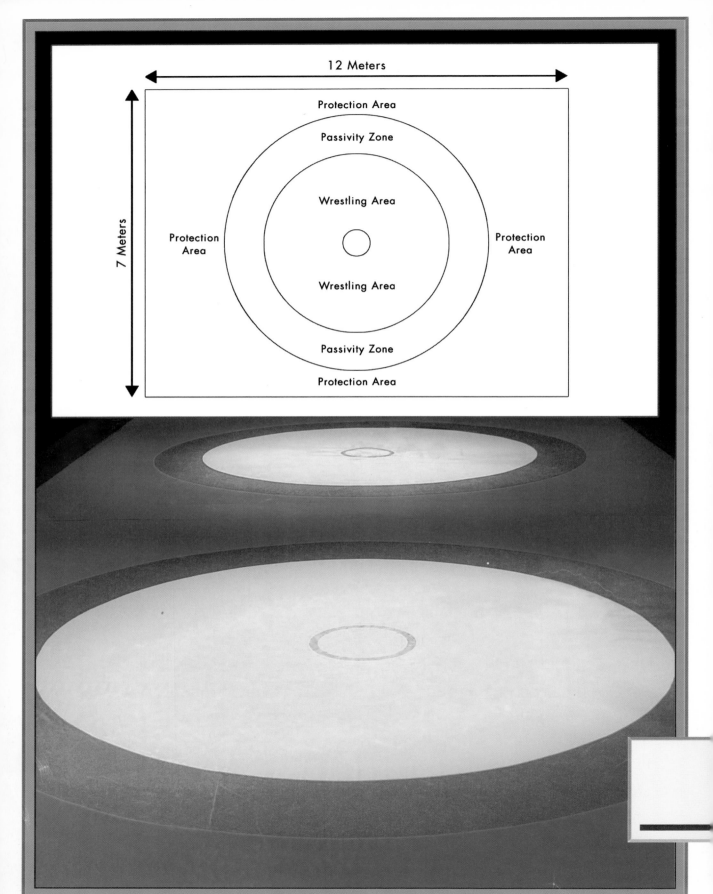

they do, the referee halts the action and tells the wrestlers to return to the center.

The Match

A wrestling match takes place on a mat with the two opponents facing each other and a referee to supervise the action. In a wrestling match, unlike in team sports, you are on your own. The main purpose is to use various moves to control your opponent. There are two ways to win a wrestling match. One is by holding your opponent's shoulders on the mat for a number of seconds. That is called a pin or a fall. You can also win by scoring the most points. The rules for both high school and college competition are similar. Before the contest begins, the wrestlers must weigh in. The weigh-in is conducted by the referee or an official. Wrestlers from opposing teams in the same weight class are paired up by a random drawing.

In high school, a match is divided into three periods lasting for two minutes each. In college, the first period lasts for three minutes, and the second and third periods last for two minutes each. In the first period, both wrestlers shake hands and begin to take their stances in the neutral position, where neither wrestler is in control. A wrestler's feet should not be touching one another. One foot must be on the starting line and the other foot behind the lead foot. The referee blows the whistle and the action begins. As both wrestlers are on their feet, they engage in hand fighting to knock

If a wrestler moves outside the line around the mat, he or she is out-of-bounds. However, a wrestler can score a takedown if his or her feet are inbounds. The double-leg drop, the single-leg sweep, the fireman's carry, the arm drag, the snapdown, and the pancake are a few kinds of takedowns.

Individual Match

In an individual competition, points for individual scores are as follows:

Takedown: 2 points; **Escape:** 1 point;
Reversal: 2 points; **Near Fall:** 2, 3, or 4 points

each other off balance. That is accomplished through early moves such as tie-ups. One wrestler will then go for a takedown, the act of bringing the opponent down to the mat from the standing position. The offensive wrestler will then try to pin the opponent's shoulders on the mat to win the match or score points by holding his opponent on his back.

The defensive wrestler will try to escape and get back to a standing position; if successful, points are awarded. If the defensive wrestler escapes and does a reversal move in which he now controls his opponent, points are gained. The referee will let the official scorer know when points are awarded. After two minutes (three minutes in college play), the referee sounds the whistle, marking the end of the first period.

The second and third periods begin with the wrestlers in the referee's position. Here the bottom, or defensive wrestler, is on his hands and knees. The knees are also behind the back starting line. The palms are flat on the mat and forward of the front starting line. The top, or offensive wrestler, has one arm around the bottom wrestler's waist with the palm on the opponent's navel. The other hand is over the opponent's elbow.

Dual Meet

The following are points awarded in a dual meet:

Fall: 6 points; **Forfeit:** 6 points; **Disqualification:** 6 points; **Technical Fall (by more than 15 points):** 5 points; **Major Decision:** 4 points; **Decision (fewer by 8 points):** 3 points

At the beginning of the second period, a coin toss determines which wrestler has a choice of being in the top, bottom, or neutral position. When the referee blows the whistle to start the second period, the offensive or top wrestler tries to break down the opponent or flatten him on the mat. The top wrestler uses whatever breakdown moves or pinning combinations are possible. Like in the first period, the defensive wrestler has to avoid being pinned down on his back or he'll either lose the match or give up points to the opponent. The referee lets the officials know which wrestler scores points. After two minutes, the whistle is blown and the action is halted.

The second wrestler has a choice of the top, bottom, or neutral position at the start of the third period. After the referee blows the whistle, the offensive wrestler will try to pin the opponent down while the defensive wrestler tries to escape the hold and reverse the play. Points for an escape or reversal are awarded to the defensive wrestler. After two minutes have elapsed, the referee ends the match. If no fall occurs, the match is decided on which wrestler scored the most points. The official scorer notifies the referee of the decision. The wrestlers are brought to the center of the circle to shake hands. The referee then raises the arm of the winner.

Referees make sure that people don't break the rules. Since wrestling is such a physical sport, it's important that someone is there to make sure players don't injure each other.

The Officials

Several people are responsible for making sure the match goes smoothly and fairly. These are the head referee, the assistant referee, the scorers, and the timekeeper.

The head referee wears a striped black-and-white shirt, black trousers, black gym shoes, and a whistle. This referee's decisions are final based on the rules. Before a match, the head referee will inspect the wrestlers to make sure they are not wearing or carrying any foreign substances or objects that are harmful to the wrestler or the opponent. The referee determines what equipment is legal, such as the uniform and mat. If necessary, he or she explains the rules to the wrestlers and the coaches. The referee also reviews the procedures with the scorers and timekeeper.

The head referee enforces penalties for violations and stops illegal holds before they become dangerous. He signals points to the scorers by using his fingers. On his left wrist he wears a red armband, and on his right wrist a green armband. The armbands are used to indicate whether the home or visiting team scored points. At the

This referee makes sure there are no violations as a high school wrestler gets pinned to the mat. The referee lifts his right hand, indicating that the visiting team has scored.

end of the match, he signs the score book from the scorers to finalize the results.

Sometimes an assistant referee is there to help the head referee. He prevents an error in judgment. However, the head referee still has the final say in a decision.

The official scorer records the points and goes over the scores at the end of the match. The scorer also speaks with the timekeeper if there is a disagreement over the score.

The timekeeper is in charge of keeping the overall time of the match. He also notifies the referee of a situation when the match is stopped or if there is a disagreement between himself and the scorer.

Scoring

In both high school and college wrestling, contestants are awarded points for both individual and team competition. With the exception of a pin (also known as a fall), in which the wrestler holds the opponent's shoulders for a number of seconds on the mat and thus ends the match, points determine the winner.

Wrestling tournaments are held at the end of the wrestling season every year. These competitions draw large crowds, as people gather to watch the intense matches and to see who will claim various school, state, and national championship titles.

Dual Meet

A dual meet is a competition between two teams. Scoring is based on the results of each individual match. For example, if a wrestler pins or falls his opponent, his team gains six points. If he scores more than fifteen points over his opponent, the match ends in a technical fall, and his team receives five points.

If both teams have the same scores at the end of a dual meet, several situations can break a tie. First, if one team has been penalized the most for flagrant misconduct, unsportsmanlike behavior, or stalling, the other team is declared the winner. Second, the team that has the most number of takedowns, reversals, or escapes is declared the winner. Third, the team that won the most matches during the meet is declared the winner.

Tournaments

At the end of the season, your team is likely to compete against other schools or wrestling clubs at a tournament. Championships from the school to national level are determined in a tournament. In it, you are likely to wrestle several competitors in one day. A tournament can be very long. You are not allowed to compete in more than five matches in one day, and you must have a forty-five-minute rest period between two consecutive matches.

Tournaments are set up in a bracket system of four, eight, or sixteen teams in a series of individual rounds. A team advances to the final round through either single elimination or double elimination. In a single elimination, two teams face each other in a round. The winning team advances to the next round and plays another winning team, while the losers are automatically eliminated. This continues until only one winner is left. In a double elimination, a team has to lose twice before being eliminated.

CHAPTER THREE

Basic Moves of Wrestling

Wrestling requires not only strength, but also a keen sense of strategy. Champion wrestlers such as Dave Schultz and John Smith relied on strategy in addition to their physical skills on the mat. To wrestle successfully, you must be able to know how to counterbalance your opponent's attack in addition to being on the offense.

Stances and Tie-Ups

At the start of the first period, the wrestlers shake hands and take their stances at the neutral position. Here, neither wrestler is in control as one faces the other. The stance allows you to be on the defensive and gives

This young wrestler lifts his opponent into the air.

you the chance to move. There are two types of stances. In the squared stance, both feet are shoulder width apart, and neither foot is forward. The staggered stance is similar to the squared stance except that one foot is in front of the other.

The referee sounds the whistle and the match begins. Now both of you will begin to make your move on each other. You are looking for an opening where you can distract your opponent and go for a takedown. A tie-up is one of those preliminary moves in the standing position that can lead to a takedown.

One kind of tie-up commonly used is the collar tie-up. The collar tie-up with inside arm control involves clamping one hand on the back of the opponent's neck while using the other hand to grab the inside of the opponent's arm.

Lifting

Lifting an opponent is an important skill as it distracts your opponent and makes him or her vulnerable. As you drive into your opponent, bend at the knees and lower your hips. Make sure you are under your opponent while grabbing him or her by the arms. Then straighten up and hoist your opponent into the air. Using your back to do this can cause you serious injury. Let your legs, hips, and thighs do the work.

Takedowns

A takedown is a move in which you bring your opponent down to the mat and control him. If the takedown is done successfully, you are awarded two points. If you score first, you will have a psychological edge throughout the match. Takedowns involve dropping to your hips and taking an aggressive forward step toward your opponent's abdominal area. Simultaneously, keep your chin up and your back straight.

One of the most common takedowns is done with a single leg. Here you shoot in low toward your opponent and wrap your arms around his or her leg. Then lift it into the air to get him or her off balance and drive your opponent onto the mat.

When you successfully perform a takedown on your opponent, you can try pinning him or her for the automatic win. Pinning is discussed later in this chapter. The referee blows his whistle, ending the first period if no pin or fall occurs.

Breakdowns

As discussed earlier, the second and third periods begin with the wrestlers in the referee's position. The defensive wrestler is on the bottom and the offensive wrestler is on top. The object for you as the top wrestler is to break down, or flatten, the opponent on his or her stomach or side. To do so, apply pressure to where your opponent has support, such as the hands or feet.

This wrestler demonstrates an effective takedown by lifting his opponent's leg. After taking down your opponent, you can score an automatic win by pinning him or her to the mat.

One popular breakdown is the cross-face, far-ankle breakdown, in which you place your left hand across your opponent's face to grasp his or her upper right arm. With the other hand, grab your opponent's right ankle and pull him or her toward you and over onto his or her shoulders.

Pinning: Nelsons and Cradles

Once you have control over your opponent on the mat, seize the opportunity to pin. Pinning is the ultimate way to win a match. In order to win, both of your opponent's shoulder blades must touch the mat for two seconds. If this is not possible, you can also score points in a near fall. This occurs when your opponent's shoulders or scapulas are held within 4 inches (10 cm) of the mat and at an angle of 45 degrees or less. If accomplished for two seconds, you are awarded two points. If you can hold the shoulders 4 inches off the mat for five seconds, you are awarded three points.

One of your pinning moves might involve a nelson. A nelson is a hold in which one hand is placed on your opponent's neck by reaching under one or both of his or her arms. You can use the half nelson if your opponent is flat on his or her stomach. Get your left hand under your opponent's left armpit and across the back of his or her neck. Hold tight your opponent's right hand with your right hand to prevent an escape. Swing your body perpendicular to his

Top: By reaching his hand underneath his opponent's arm, the offensive wrestler puts his opponent in a nelson. *Bottom:* A wrestler puts his opponent in a cradle and forces him onto his back.

or hers and drive your legs in so you end up chest to chest with your opponent.

Cradles are maneuvers useful in pinning. One example is the near-side cradle in which you place your left arm across your opponent's neck. Then use your right hand and place it under his or her left knee. Lock hands and drive your head into your opponent's ribcage while lifting his or her other knee. Then force your opponent over onto his or her back.

Escapes

Learning how to escape from your opponent can be the difference between success and failure. An escape, worth one point, is a move in which you are able to free yourself and get back into the neutral position. A reversal is a move in which you switch from the bottom position to the top position. You go from being controlled by to controlling your opponent. If the move is done successfully, you are awarded two points.

One way to escape is to execute the stand-up. Shift your weight into your opponent's body and grab your opponent's left wrist with your right hand as you try to get up. Lock elbows so your opponent can't reach in under your arms. Get up on your left foot in front of your right leg and thrust your entire body upward. Use your hands to pull your opponent's hand off your waist.

Illegal Holds and Infractions

As in other sports, wrestling has rules that must be followed to prevent injury to yourself or to your opponent. You can lose points or be disqualified if they are not followed.

Honoring Wrestling Greats

The National Wrestling Hall of Fame and Museum, located in Stillwater, Oklahoma, was founded in 1976. It honors the greatest wrestlers in the sport and houses memorabilia from wrestling's past. Here are a few great wrestlers and some of their career highlights.

Dan Gable had a combined prep and college record of 181 wins and 1 loss. His greatest moment was at the 1972 Olympics in Munich, Germany, where he defeated all six opponents without giving up a single point.

Dave Schultz collected ten national championships. He won an Olympic gold medal in 1984 by defeating his opponents with a combined score of 42 to 2.

Bruce Baumgartner had a record of 134 wins and 12 losses, including pinning his opponents 73 times in his college career. He would go on to become World Champion in 1986, 1993, and 1995. In the 1984 Olympics, Bruce became the first American in 60 years to win a gold medal in the super heavyweight class.

John Smith became known for his quick single-leg takedown that made him unstoppable. His combined career record was 436 wins, 20 losses, and 2 ties, a winning rate of more than 95 percent.

Rulon Gardner's Greco-Roman wrestling accomplishments included winning the World Cup in 1996 and capturing the Pan American championship and the Vantaa Cup, both in 1998. His greatest win was defeating the legendary wrestler Aleksandr Karelin of Russia in the 2000 Olympics. Karelin had not lost a match in thirteen years, and had not given up a point in ten years.

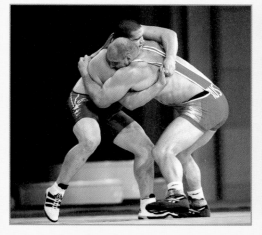

Rulon Gardner (*left*) grapples with Aleksandr Karelin (*right*).

This wrestler traps his unfortunate opponent in a full nelson. A full nelson is an illegal move because it can permanently injure someone. It's good to be competitive when you wrestle, but it's also important to have good sportsmanship.

Certain holds on the mouth, nose, throat, or neck that restrict breathing or circulation are banned. Some examples include the full nelson, body slams, and strangleholds. The first and second penalties are worth one point each, the third penalty is worth two points, and the fourth penalty carries a disqualification.

Stalling is another violation. It occurs when a wrestler is intentionally wasting time by staying out of bounds, playing at the edge of the mat, or not attempting to wrestle. In college matches, the offending wrestler will receive a warning after the first violation, and will be penalized a point for the second and third time it occurs. After a two-point penalty for the fourth violation, he or she will be disqualified from the match if called for a fifth time.

Unsportsmanlike conduct is not tolerated. Examples include ignoring the referee's warnings and shoving, taunting, swearing, and intimidating your opponent. Flagrant misconduct includes biting, striking, and kicking an opponent. If the misconduct is considered serious by the referee, the wrestler will be removed from the premises and his team will lose points.

If one wrestler injures his or her opponent using an illegal hold and he or she cannot continue the match, the injured wrestler wins by default. If a wrestler intentionally injures the opponent, the wrestler will be disqualified. If a wrestler is accidentally injured and cannot carry on, his or her opponent wins.

CHAPTER FOUR

Equipment, Preparation, and Getting Involved

Wearing the proper safety gear will help protect you from injury.

Wrestling requires little equipment. You can start out by wearing gym clothes and sneakers. As you progress in your training and participate in competition, you will need some special gear. Most sporting goods stores and Web sites sell wrestling clothes and equipment.

Clothes

A wrestler wears a singlet, a one-piece, close-fitting nylon uniform that extends from the shoulders to the thighs. Singlets are usually worn during tournaments. Much like uniforms in other sports, the singlets come in colors representing the wrestler's school or organization.

Shoes

Wrestling shoes should be lightweight and reach up to the ankle. They should be rubber soled and heelless, and should have some form of traction. A good wrestling shoe should allow stability, flexibility, and support for quick maneuvers.

Headgear or Ear Guards

Headgear or ear guards are required during practice and competition. This is for protection of the ears, where injuries are most common. Cushioned ear cups are held in place by a buckle-free strap to prevent a ruptured eardrum.

Knee Pads

Wearing knee pads is optional, although they offer protection against getting bruised, worn knees.

Weight Requirements

All competitors must weigh in before a wrestling match begins to ensure fairness of competition. The weights are recorded by the official scorer. Afterward, the contestants in the same weight classification

Nutrition Requirements for the Aspiring Wrestler

As in any sport, wrestling requires that you eat the right foods. A well-balanced diet ensures good physical and mental health. According to a study by the Center for Nutrition in Sport and Human Performance conducted for the NCAA, this consists of foods containing the following.

Carbohydrates make up for lost energy burned during play, and they stimulate muscle growth. Foods rich in carbohydrates include potatoes, cereal, bread, pasta, and fresh fruit. Your intake of carbohydrates should be about 60 percent of your total caloric intake.

Fats from sources like soybean oil, olive oil, and canola oil also provide a source of energy. Good fats should make up from 20 to 30 percent of your caloric intake.

Proteins are the essential building blocks of muscles, blood, skin, hair, and tissues. Proteins can be found in foods such as meat, fish, skim milk, poultry, and legumes. A normal diet should consist of about 20 percent protein.

Minerals such as calcium and iron are also essential in maintaining good health. Calcium keeps your bones strong. Foods such as leafy green vegetables (spinach, kale) and milk contain calcium. Iron maintains the healthy red blood cells that carry oxygen to your body. Meat, fish, fruits, and greens are rich in iron.

Water is essential before, during, and after play. When you wrestle, you sweat, and your body loses water. You should drink about 20 ounces (59 cl) of water two hours before practice and 8 ounces (24 cl) every 15 to 20 minutes during practice.

Some wrestlers will starve or dehydrate themselves in order to maintain their weight level. Although they think this will help them be better wrestlers, they are actually damaging their bodies.

are paired through a random draw. In high school, wrestlers can belong to fourteen different weight classes, ranging from 103 pounds (47 kg) to 275 pounds (125 kg). For college competitions, the weight classes vary from 125 pounds (57 kg) to 183 to 285 pounds (83 to 129 kg).

The Dangers of Rapid Weight Loss

Some wrestlers feel pressure to lose weight so that they can stay within their proper weight class and gain an edge. Some wear a rubber suit in which to sweat and, therefore, shed pounds. Still others use more extreme measures such as vomiting or starving themselves. Drugs and nutritional supplements have also been used as weight loss aids. All these methods are illegal and very dangerous to the health of a wrestler. Excessive weight loss leads to tiredness, mood swings, short-term memory loss, and even death. In 1997, three college wrestlers died trying to make weight requirements for competition. You should consult your doctor or nutritionist on how to maintain your ideal weight.

Training and Conditioning

A good conditioning program strengthens your body and promotes good health. Stretching your upper and lower body loosens the muscles, lubricates the joints, and gets the blood flowing. It also decreases your chance for serious injury and discomfort during play. According to Nick Ugoalah, fitness trainer and Canadian freestyle champion, wrestlers need to spend from ten to fifteen minutes warming up. Such warm-up exercises include running, skipping rope, or using a stair climber. They should be followed by basic stretches for the lower and upper parts of your body. Stretching exercises for the lower portion of your body should include the hamstrings, quadraceps, groin, and calf muscles. These involve holding a part of your leg for about a minute to get a good stretch and then working on the other leg. Upper-body stretches for your arms and back should involve arm circles, push-ups, sit-ups, and pull-ups. For these, you should start out with a few repetitions and then gradually increase them.

Weight training should be part of your program as it helps build muscle strength and mass. At your gymnasium or fitness club, you can find weight-training equipment such as free weights, dumbbells, and nautilus machines. Younger children who have not reached puberty should not weight train strenuously because it can harm their skeletal development. If you use the weights properly, you will avoid sprains and injury.

Involvement in other sports and physical activities, or cross training, is beneficial. It will strengthen your muscles while improving your hand-eye coordination and mobility.

Before taking on any rigorous strength and conditioning program, have a checkup from your doctor. Also talk to fitness instructors about what program is suitable for your body.

These wrestlers are limbering up before wrestling. You should stretch for at least ten to fifteen minutes before a match to avoid muscle pulls. *Inset:* A wrestler stretches his groin.

How to Get Involved

You can start wrestling at an early age. Many schools across the country offer wrestling as part of high school sports. There are also youth wrestling clubs and camps that offer individual and group instruction.

One way to introduce yourself to the sport is by watching a wrestling match on television, such as the Olympics. There are also instructional videos that describe the methods and techniques used. You can find these at your video store, library, or online.

Another way to build interest in the sport is to attend a wrestling match. Find out if your school, college, or local athletic club has wrestling practices and matches. You can learn a lot by observing how the match is conducted and studying the types of moves used. Talk to coaches and wrestlers to get a feel for what competing is like.

If you want to participate in wrestling, find out which organizations and schools in your area have wrestling programs. Contact your library, consult your phone book, or go online to see if there is a wrestling club for kids. If you are fourteen years or older, contact the National Federation of State High School Associations (NFHS), the governing body of high school athletics, to find out which high schools in your state have a wrestling program. You can also contact USA Wrestling for information on sanctioned wrestling associations and clubs in your state.

Wrestling Camps

If you cannot find a local youth or high school level wrestling program in your area, you may want to consider traveling to an overnight youth camp. There are many wrestling camps all over the United States. Some even have programs for women. Most camps are held during the summer, and the duration of the program can last from a few days to a week. Some former stars like Bruce Baumgartner run their own camps, bringing their unique styles to aspiring wrestlers.

To find out about wrestling camps in your area, consult the phone book or library. Most wrestling camps have Web sites. Contact USA Wrestling to find certified and recommended camps.

Wrestling camps are a great way to train to become a wrestler if you do not have a local or high school wrestling program. These camps provide instruction about wrestling techniques, the chance to practice those techniques with other campers, and the opportunity to review what you've learned in drills.

College and Beyond

At some colleges, particularly in the Midwest, wrestling is a major part of the athletic programs. Institutions such as Iowa State, Oklahoma State, and the University of Nebraska traditionally have championship wrestling teams that compete for the NCAA title. Some schools offer wrestling scholarships depending on athletic and

Wrestling can help you develop both mental and physical discipline. It helps develop a healthy sense of competition and self-esteem. Even though it is a game of physical dominance, the most important thing about wrestling is having fun.

academic ability. College wrestling coaches scout and recruit high school athletes that show promise for their programs.

Beyond college, amateur wrestlers compete in national championships, such as the USAW Senior Freestyle Championships, and international tournaments, such as the World Championships and the Olympics. To participate in the World Championships and the Olympics as a representative of the United States, competitors have to be sponsored by USA Wrestling. In order to qualify to be on the U.S. Olympic team, you must attend tryouts. Spots are won through competition. Even 2000 Olympic gold medalist Rulon Gardner had to earn his place on the 2004 team.

Wrestling is a demanding sport that requires a strong work ethic, endurance, and energy. Although physical strength is very important, being clever and smart can help you get an edge over your opponent. Unlike other sports, wrestling doesn't require much equipment, additional players, or being six feet tall and huge. It is a safe and fun activity that builds self-esteem and confidence, promotes health and fitness, and fosters a competitive spirit. It is the sense of one-on-one competition and overcoming adversity that makes wrestling an appealing and enduring sport. With hard work and a good understanding of the techniques involved, you can become a successful wrestler.

GLOSSARY

breakdown   A move in which the offensive wrestler flattens his or her opponent on his or her stomach or side.

cradle   A maneuver that sets up for a pin in which one wrestler wraps his or her arms on the back of the opponent's neck and legs and then locks his or her hands.

fall   To hold your opponent on his or her back with both of his or her shoulders touching the mat for two seconds.

folkstyle   A style of wrestling practiced from elementary school to college in which opponents are permitted to use their arms, legs, and bodies to secure holds to either win by a pin or by scoring points.

freestyle   A style of wrestling, similar to folkstyle, in which opponents are permitted to use their arms, legs, and bodies to secure holds to either win by a pin or by scoring points, though different in scoring and strategy.

Greco-Roman wrestling   A style of wrestling in which the wrestlers are not allowed to use their legs during the action.

pin   The act of holding your opponent's shoulders on the mat for two seconds to win the match.

singlet   A close-fitting spandex or nylon one-piece uniform worn by wrestlers.

sumo   A type of Japanese wrestling.

FOR MORE INFORMATION

The Dave Schultz Wrestling Club
P.O. Box 4418
Cambridge, MA 94404
Web site: http://schultzwrestling.org

National Federation of State High School Associations (NFHS)
P.O. Box 690
Indianapolis, IN 46206
Web site: http://www.nfhs.org

National Wrestling Hall of Fame and Museum
405 W. Hall of Fame
Stillwater, OK 74075
Web site: http://www.wrestlinghalloffame.com

United States Olympic Committee
National Headquarters
One Olympic Plaza
Colorado Springs, CO 80909
Web site: http://www.olympic-usa.org

USA Wrestling
6155 Lehman Drive
Colorado Springs, CO 80918
Web site: http://www.themat.com/newusaw

Web Sites

Due to the changing nature of Internet links, the Rosen Publishing Group, Inc., has developed an on-line list of Web sites related to the subject of this book. This site is updated regularly. Please use this link to access the list:

http://www.rosenlinks.com/scc/wres

FOR FURTHER READING

Angle, Kurt, with John Harper. *It's True! It's True!* New York: Regan Books, 2001.

Dellinger, Bob. "Changing of the Guard." National Wrestling Hall of Fame and Museum. Retrieved August 18, 2003 (http://www.wrestlinghalloffame.org).

Mysnyk, Mark, Barry Davis, and Brooks Simpson. *Winning Wrestling Moves.* Champaign, IL: Human Kinetics, 1994.

BIBLIOGRAPHY

Dellinger, Bob. "The Oldest Sport." National Wrestling Hall of Fame and Museum. Retrieved August 18, 2003 (http://www.wrestlinghalloffame.org).

Dellinger, Bob. "Wrestling in the USA." National Wrestling Hall of Fame and Museum. Retrieved August 18 2003 (http://www.wrestlinghalloffame.org).

Diehl, Jerry L., ed. *2003-2004 NFHS Wrestling Rules Book.* Indianapolis: NFHS Publications, 2003.

Gable, Dan. "Wrestling." *World Book Encyclopedia.* Chicago: World Book, 2003.

Gallagher, Jim. *The Composite Guide to Wrestling.* Philadelphia: Chelsea House, 1998.

Periello, Vito. A., M.D. "Aiming for a Healthy Weight in Wrestlers and other Athletes." *Contemporary Pediatrics*, September 2001, pp. 55–74.

Ryan, Thomas, and Julie Sampson. *Beginning Wrestling.* New York: Sterling, 2002.

Sullivan, George. *Better Wrestling for Boys.* New York: Putnam Publishing Group, 1986.

"Wrestling." Encyclopaedia Britannica. 2003. Retrieved October 16, 2003 (http://search.eb.com/eb/article?eu=79631).

INDEX

About the Author

David Chiu is a freelance writer living in New York City.

Photo Credits

Cover (group, mat, and wrestler on the right), pp. 1 (wrestlers on the left and right), 3, 5, 13, 18, 22, 23, 25, 27, 30, 32 (wrestler, shoes, and knee pads), 33, 35, 37 Nancy Opitz; cover (wrestlers on the left) © Ed Zurga/AP/World Wide Photos; p. 4 © Alinari Archives/Corbis; pp. 7, 8, 9 Hulton Archive/Getty Images; p. 10 © Chris Trotman/New Sport/Corbis; p. 12 © Dimitri Iundt/Corbis; p. 14 © Photo & Co./Corbis; pp. 19, 20 © AP/Wide World Photos; p. 29 © Corbis Sygma; pp. 39, 40 Getty Images.

Thanks to Midwood Wrestling Team, Midwood High School, Brooklyn, New York.

Designer: Nelson Sá; **Editor:** Leigh Ann Cobb; **Photo Researcher:** Rebecca Anguin-Cohen.